W. M. HAWLEY

CHINESE FOLK DESIGNS

**A COLLECTION OF 300 CUT-PAPER DESIGNS
USED FOR EMBROIDERY**

Together with

160 CHINESE ART SYMBOLS

and their meanings

DOVER PUBLICATIONS, INC.
NEW YORK

中國剪紙
藝術選集

Published in Canada by General Publishing Company, Ltd., 30 Lesmill
Road, Don Mills, Toronto, Ontario.
Published in the United Kingdom by Constable and Company, Ltd.,
10 Orange Street, London WC 2.

This Dover edition, first published in 1971, is an unabridged republication
of the work originally published by the author in 1949.

DOVER *Pictorial Archive* SERIES

International Standard Book Number: 0-486-22633-6
Library of Congress Catalog Card Number: 77-179790

Manufactured in the United States of America
Dover Publications, Inc.
180 Varick Street
New York, N. Y. 10014

A WORD ABOUT THE *HUA YANG* 花樣 PATTERNS

This book achieves the impossible in that it presents an entirely untouched and long ignored aspect of Oriental art: paper cutting.

Since the Mongol Dynasty, scholars and scientists of every race and persuasion - lay and religious - have returned from China with examples of that nation's skills; few have so much as made reference to the subject covered in this book.

The Chinese themselves totally neglected to include this art, in this utilitarian phase, in their exhaustive art literature, perhaps because of its obvious peasant origin - - - and because primarily it is only an intermediate step in the production of what they consider a superior handicraft: their rich embroideries.

Chinese embroidery patterns fall into two categories - - - those which are sketched, a device used on larger projects, and the *hua yang* which are used for small articles of everyday use: women's and children's footwear, children's caps and dresses, aprons . . . It is the *hua yang* with which we are herein concerned.

The *hua yang* designs are cut freehand with scissors, as we cut silhouettes, but perhaps a stack of several at one time. Most are so intricate as to preclude more than a very few being produced at one cutting. However, coarser designs are turned out in some volume by the use of chisels and small knives. Plate 248 shows this method.

It is not known where these cut paper designs originated, the date of their beginning, or when they first were adapted to the delicate needs of the embroiderer. Evidence exists that they have been in common use for many centuries. Prototypes, still found in every Chinese province and village, are the red and gilt paper charms and household gods of festive and ritual use, particularily in evidence during the New Year celebrations. *Hua yang* from *Honan* (247 - 256) show the connecting link, being adaptable to both purposes: pasting on silk to embroider over, or on walls as charms. Reproductions are full size.

This exceptionally fine collection was gathered by *Wang Li-an* and *Huang Chung* over a period of years, from the following Southern and Eastern provinces - - - *Kiangsu* plates 1 - 151, *Chekiang* 152 - 206, *Kiangsi* 207-246, *Honan* 247-256, *Kweichou* 257-260, *Anhwei* 261 - 300.

It is hoped that this presentation will furnish new inspiration to students in many fields of artistic endeavor.

W. M. Hawley
September 1949.

INDEX TO THE SUBJECTS REPRESENTED

See the Supplement for additional symbols and their significance.

1. Dragon chasing the Pearl.
Symbol of the Emperor, Eternity, Beneficial forces of nature.

2. Plum blossom.
Symbol of Winter.

3. Butterfly and Flower.

4. Flower.

5. Flower.

6. Butterflies
Symbol of Joy, Wedded bliss.

7. Flower.

8. Flower basket.
Emblem of the Patron Saint of Florists.

9. Phoenix.
Symbol of the Empress, Beauty, Peace, Prosperity, Sun.

10. a. *Shou* 壽, Coins, Bat: Long life, Wealth, Happiness.
b. Flower pattern.

11. Lobster.

12. Tangerine.

13. Lion playing with balls.
Valor, Power.

14. Cock and chrysanthemum.

15. Boat and sunrise.

16. Parrot.

17. Flower.

18. Butterfly.

19. Chinese cabbage.

20. Dragons and pearl.

21. Mandarin ducks.

22. Flower basket.

23. a. Bird pattern.
    b. *Hsi* 喜 and butterfly; Joy.

24. Camellia.

25. Pomegranite.

26. Hen.

27. Flower.

28. Flower and butterfly.

29. A junk.

30. *Hydrangea flower.*

31. Phoenixes and flower.

32. Boys with lanterns in a garden.

33. Swastika: The mind.

34. Serpent.

35. Flower basket.

36. a. Swastika and flowers.
    b. Pavilion.

37. Goldfish.

38. Citron.
Fu Shou 手佛 Buddha's hand; Wealth.

39. Sparrow.

40. Flower.

41. Flower and insect.

42. *Li Hua* 李花 Plum blossom.

43. Bird and flower.

44 The phoenix singing to the rising sun.
Feng Ming Chao Yang 鳳鳴朝陽.
Talent succeeds at the proper time.

45.Flower.

46. Dragon and pearl.

47. Flower basket.

48. **Phoenix** and *Shou* 壽.
Symbol of goodness, beauty and long life.

49. Goldfish.

50. A pink.

51. Plum blossom and magpie.

52. Butterfly and chrysanthemum.

53. Flower.

54 Lion and balls.

55. Magpie and barberry.

56. Barberry.

57. Butterfly.

58. Flower and magpie.

59. Dragon and pearl.

60. Flower basket.

61. a. Swastika: The mind at peace.
   b. Longevity and wealth.
   c. Sacred jewel: Beauty and purity.

62. Fighting cocks.

63. Flower.

64. Bamboo and butterfly.

65. Flower.

66. Grapes and phoenix.

67. Flower.

68. Flower basket.

69. Eagle preying on a chicken.

70. Plum blossom.

71. Crab.

72. The Cowherd, *Ch'ien Niu* 牽牛, meets his love, the Spinning Maiden, *Chih Nü* 織女, on the Bridge of Magpies which spans the Milky Way on the 7th day of the 7th moon.

73. Flower.

74. Flower.

75. Flower and butterfly.

76. Flower.

77. Cock preying on a centipede.

78. Flower.

79. Flower.

80. The Immortal *Liu Hai* 劉海 playing with gold coins and the three legged toad. A symbol of good fortune.

81. Dragon and phoenix.
Emblems of the Emperor and Empress.

82. Grapes.

83. Bird and boat.

84. Chinese guitar and flower.

85. Chrysanthemum.

86. Water buffalo.

87. Butterfly and flower.

88. Two magpies.

89. *Ssu Chi An Lo* 四季安樂.
A wish for happiness throughout the Four Seasons.

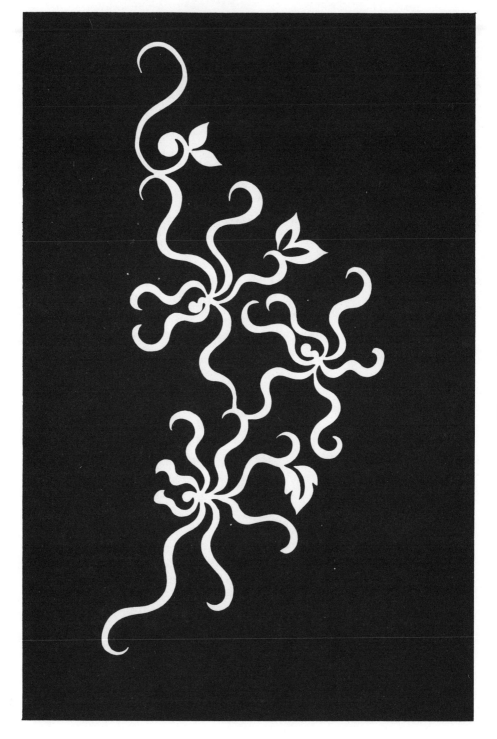

90. Chrysanthemums.

91. Flower and dragon-fly.

92. Flower.

93. Dragon and tiger fighting.

94. Flower.

95. Flower and rat.

96. Flower.

97. Chrysanthemum.

98. Water-lily, bats and coins.
Symbol of purity, long life and wealth.

99. Crane

100. Three *Shou* 壽 characters; long life.

101. Flower.

102 Dragon and phoenix.

103. Citron and flower.

104. Goldfish.

105. Flower.

106 Squirrel and grapes.

107. Two cranes.

108. *Shou* 壽, bats and coins.
Longevity and prosperity.

109. Toad and coins; wealth.

110. Flower.

111. Flower.

112. a. Sheep.
b. 5 venomous things; tiger, snake, lizard, centipede, spider.

113. Mandarin ducks and flower.

114. *Ch'u Men Chien T'sai* 出門見財.
Venture forth if you would find your fortune.

115. Snake devouring a frog.

116. Pumpkin and butterfly.

117. Flower.

118. Crane.

119. Barberry.

120. *Shou* 壽, bat and butterfly.
Symbol of long life and joy.

121. Cat.

122. Goose.

123. Flowers.

124. Flower.

125. Flower.

126. Phoenix.

127. Rabbit and flower.

128. Flower.

129. Horn cup, lotus pods and swastika.
Symbol of happiness and fruitfulness.

130. Plum blossom.

131. Crane.

132. Flower.

133. Magpie.

134. Flower.

135. Tiger and rabbit.

136. Pheasants.

137. Lark and chicken.

138. Horse.

139. Magpie.

140. Falling flowers.

141. Flowers.

142. Flower.

143. Flower.

144. Birds kissing.

145. Chrysanthemum.

146. Mandarin ducks.

147. Plum blossom.

148. Flower.

149. Flower.

150. Cormorant.

151. Lotus charm.

152. Bat.

153. Boat.

154. Phoenix.

155. Dragon.

156. Flower.

157. Flower.

158. Water buffalo.

159. Flower.

160. Turnips.

161. Wasps and chrysanthemum.

162. Phoenix.

163. Flowers.

164. Landscape.

165. Frog and fly.

166. a. **Dragon**
   b. *Shou* 壽 and five bats: Age, wealth, health, virtue.

167. Deer.

168. Landscape.

169. Carp.

170. Monkey.

171. Landscape.

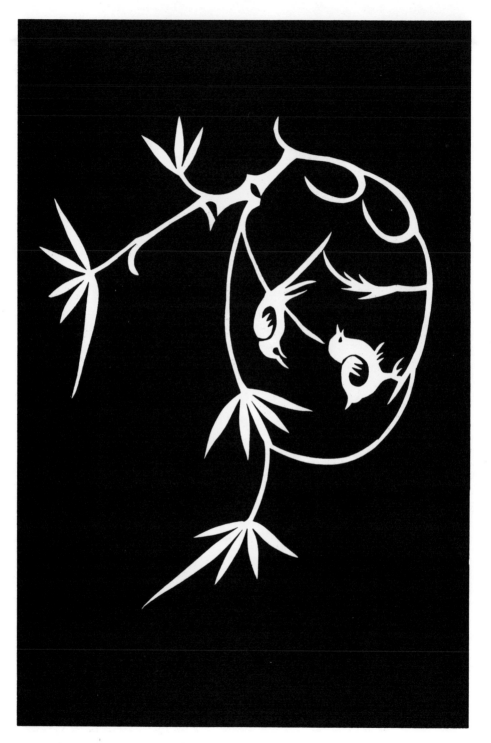

172. Thrush and chicken.

173. Butterflies.

174. Dragon.

175. Citron.

176. Pig.

177. Landscape.

178. Dragonflies.

179. Flower.

180. Goldfish.

181. Flower.

182. Landscape.

183. Flower.

184. Shrimp and flower.

185. Unicorn.

186. Landscape.

187. Flower.

188. Landscape.

189. Flower.

190. Landscape.

191. Flower.

192. Shrimps.

193. Flower.

194. Landscape.

195. Landscape.

196. Landscape.

197. Flower.

198. Horse.

199. a. Squirrel and grapes.
b. Flower.

200. Landscape.

201. Boat in moonlight.

202. Landscape.

203. Three rabbits.

204. Flower.

205. Flower.

206. Flower and *Shou* 壽 Longevity.

207. Duck.

208. Bat and chrysanthemum.

209. *Chiang T'ai-kung* 姜太公 fishing in the *Wei* river while awaiting Emperor *Wen* 文 who made him a statesman at 80.

210. Carp.

211. Flower.

212. Flower.

213. Flower.

214. Peach. Symbol of Immortality, Marriage, Springtime.

215. Flower.

216. Flower.

217. Flower.

218. Chinese persimmon.

219. Barberry.

220. Flower.

221. Lotus.

222. Flower.

223. Flower.

224. Flat beans.

225. Orchid.

226. Bamboo and dragonfly.

227. Chinese cabbage.

230. Carp leaping the Dragon Gate to become dragons.
Symbol of success through overcoming great obstacles.

231. Flower.

232. Flower.

233. Flower.

234. Flower.

235. Flower.

236. Unicorn.

237. a. Citron and bat.
b. Mallow.

238. Chrysanthemum.

239. New moon.

240. Flowers.

241. Flower.

242. Flower.

243. Flower.

244. Dog and lotus.

245. Flower.

246. Flower.

247. Flower.

248. Scepter *Ju-i* 如意.
Contentment, Prosperity.

249. *Chao T'sai Chin Pao* 招財進寶, a charm to bring wealth.

250. *Huang Chin Wan Liang* 黃金萬兩.
A charm to bring 10,000 ounces of gold.

251. *Fu Shou Shuang Ch'üan* 福壽雙全.
A charm to insure prosperity and long life.

252. A pair of fish: Symbol of conjugal felicity.

253. *Fu Kuei Yu Yü* 富貴有餘(魚).
A charm to insure a surplus of wealth.

254. *Nien Nien Ju I* 年年如意.
A charm to provide satisfaction year by year.

255. *Huang Chin Wan Liang* 黃金萬兩.
A charm to bring 10,000 ounces of gold.

256. *Ssu Chi Fa Ts'ai* 四季發財.
A charm to provide good fortune in the Four Seasons.

257. A bridal chair.

258. The *Yang Yin* 陽陰 and *Pa Kua* 八卦 symbols.

259. *Shou* 壽 and 5 bats: Longevity, wealth, virtue.

260. Monkey.

261. Bird and ox.

262. *Chu Ko-liang* 諸葛亮.
A notorious statesman of the *San Kuo* 三國 period.

263. *Shou* 壽 Longevity.

264. Goldfish.

265. *Chi Kung* 濟公.
A mysterious mad monk of the *Sung* dynasty.

266. Carp.

267. *Kuan Yü* 關羽 a famous general of the *San Kuo* period.

268. Flower.

269. Squirrels.

270. *Mi Lo Fu* 彌勒佛 the Buddha Maitreya.
The patron saint of goldsmiths and silversmiths.

271. *Kuan Yin* 觀音 the Goddess of Mercy and her disciple.

272. *Ch'ang Wo* 嫦娥 fleeing to the moon. She was the wife of the tyrant *I* 羿 and stole the drug of Immortality from him. He ordered her death, but she was able to mount to heaven.

273. *Ts'ai Shen* 財神 the God of Wealth.

274. *Shou Hsing* 壽星 the God of Longevity.

275. The Buddha Amoghapasa, the 8 armed *Kuan Yin*.

276. The *T'ang* Emperor *Ming* 明 visits the moon for pleasure.

277. *Wu Sung* 武松 *beats the tiger which had terrified the people of Mount Ching Yang.*

278. Flowers.

279. *Wei Cheng* 魏徵 a politition of the *T'ang* dynasty.

280. *Su Wu* 蘇武 as a shepherd. A *Han* statesman who was
sent as an envoy, he was held and banished to sheep herding.

281. A fairy scattering flowers. Buddha once ordered flowers
scattered over his assembled disciples proving that he to whom
the flowers adhered was a slave of his passions.

282. Boy among flowers.

283. *Mu Lan* 木蘭, disguised as a man, joins the army serving 12 years in place of her old father. Symbol of filial piety.

284. *Lien Sheng Kuei Tzu* 連(蓮)生貴子 a play on words.
"To give birth to a succession of noble boys."

285. *Su San* 蘇三 in extradition. A famous courtesan who helped her lover and was later freed by his aid.

286. *Yang Ssu-lang* 楊四郎 visits his mother. A *Sung* general invading *Liao*, he was captured. The Queen *Hsiao* 蕭 admiring his bravery, made him her son-in-law. Later, becoming home-sick, his wife arranged for him to go home for a visit.

287. Tiger and *Shou* 壽 Bravery and Longevity.

288. *Chung-li Ch'üan* 鍾離權 Chief of the Eight Immortals.
He has the Elixer of Life and the Power of Transmutation.

289. *Ho Hsien-ku* 何仙姑 one of the Eight Immortals.
Female sage who assists in household management.

290. *Lan Ts'ai-ho* 藍采和 one of the Eight Immortals.
Symbol of delusive pleasures, patron saint of florists.

291. *Ts'ao Kuo-chiu* 曹國舅 one of the Eight Immortals.
Patron saint of the theater.

292. *Han Hsiang-tzu* 韓湘子 one of the Eight Immortals.
Patron saint of musicians.

293. *Li T'ieh-kuai* 李鐵拐 one of the Eight Immortals.
A magician. Emblems; an iron crutch and gourd.

294. *Lü Tung-pin* 呂洞賓 one of the Eight Immortals.
Patron of barbers. Slays dragons, checks evil, cures the sick.

295. *Chang Kuo-lao* 張果老 one of the Eight Immortals.
Emblem; bamboo drum. He rode a white mule backwards.

296. The monk *Hsüan-chuang* 玄奘 of the *T'ang* dynasty.
He made pilgrimages westward to get the Buddhist Sutras.

297. *Sun Wu-k'ung* 孫悟空 the Monkey Spirit.
First disciple escorting the monk *Hsüan Chuang* on his travels.

298. *Chu Wu-neng* 豬悟能 the Pig Spirit.
Second disciple and escort of *Hsuan Chuang* on his travels.

299. *Sha Wu-ching* 沙悟淨 the Shark Spirit.
Third disciple and escort of *Hsüan Chuang* on his travels.

300. *Ch'i-lin* 麒麟 or Unicorn carrying a boy child.
A charm to insure male offspring.

中國美術表號

CHINESE ART SYMBOLS

160 Symbols Commonly Used in the Decoration of Art Objects with
their Symbolical Meanings Drawn from the Chinese Originals for
ORIENTAL CULTURE CHART # 12
by Francess Hawley Seyssel

The *Yang Yin* 陽陰 and *Pa Kua* 八卦 symbols.

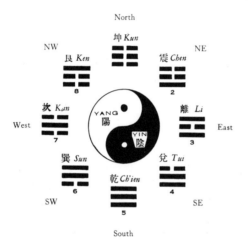

The *Pa Kua* or Eight Trigrams.

#	Direction	Zodiac	Symbolism
1.	North	Ox	Earth, capaciousness, submission.
2.	NE	Dragon	Thunder, moving exciting power.
3.	East	Pheasant	Fire, sun, lightening, brightness, elegance.
4.	SE	Goat	Still water, pleasure, complacent satisfaction.
5.	South	Horse	Heaven, power, untiring strength.
6.	SW	Cock	Wind, wood, penetration, flexibility.
7.	West	Pig	Moving water, moon, rain, difficulty, peril.
8.	NW	Dog	Mountains, hills, resting, arresting.

The *Yang Yin* or Dual Principle in Nature.

Yang - Light, heaven, sun, male, vigour, penetration, odd numbers.

Yin - Dark, earth, moon, female, quiet, absorption, even numbers.

陽陰 **Yang Yin**
1. Dual Principle

八卦 **Pa Kua**
2. 8 Trigrams

璧面 **Shên Mien**
3. Sacred Disc

壽 **Shou**
4. Longevity

1. The *Yang Yin* is the Mystic Dual Principle that represents the inter-action of opposites in Nature. The light portion, *Yang*, takes in Heaven, Sun, Light, Vigor, Male, Penetration, Dragon, Monad, Azure color, Mountains, Odd numbers. The dark half, *Yin*, represents the Earth, Moon, Dark, Quiescence, Female, Absorption, Tiger, Orange color, Duad, Valleys, Even numbers.
2. The Eight Trigrams are used in divination. See diagram opposite.
3. The Sacred Disc is the *Pa Kua* in motion, Heavenly Perfection.
4. The character *Shou* in many conventionalized and fancy forms is used to offer wishes for a long life.

福 **Fu**
5. Prosperity

祿 **Lu**
6. Riches

囍 **Hsi** (喜喜)
7. Double Joy

萬 **Wan**
8. Swastika

5, 6. Fanciful forms of *Fu*, Prosperity and *Lu*, Riches.
7. *Hsi*, Joy, doubled to symbolize Married Happiness.   Many forms.
8. The Swastika represents the Heart of the Buddha Shakyamuni, Resignation of Spirit, all Happiness that humanity desires, Mind, Infinity, All, Many, 10,000.
Blue Swastika - Infinite Celestial Virtues.
Red Swastika - Infinite Sacred Virtues of the Heart of Buddha.
Yellow Swastika - Infinite Prosperity.
Green Swastika - Infinite Virtues of Agriculture.

ANIMALS OF THE ZODIAC

鼠 **Shu**
9. Rat

牛 **Niu**
10. Ox

虎 **Hu**
11. Tiger

兔 **T'u**
12. Hare

9. The Rat represents North in the Zodiac Compass.
10. The Ox represses Evil Spirits that disturb lakes, rivers, and seas.
11. The Tiger represents Strength, Military Prowess and is one of the four animals symbolizing Power and Energy. The White Tiger presides over the Western Quadrant of the Heavens.
12. The Hare is a symbol of Longevity and East.

龍 **Lung**
13. Dragon

蛇 **Shê**
14. Serpent

馬 **Ma**
15. Horse

羊 **Yang**
16. Goat

13. The Dragon represents Royalty, Rain, Spring. He presides over the Eastern Quadrant and admonishes against Greed and Avarice.
14. The Serpent symbolizes Cunning, Evil, and Supernatural Power.
15. The Horse occupies the position of South on the compass.
16. The Goat or Sheep represents Sacrifice; the lamb, Filial Piety.

猴 **Hou**
17. Monkey

雞 **Chi**
18. Cock

犬 **Ch'uan**
19. Dog

豕 **Shih**
20. Boar

17. The Monkey drives away Evil Spirits.
18. The Cock is Courageous, has a Warlike Disposition, and represents the Warmth and Life of the Universe. Occupies the West.
19. The Dog is a symbol of Future Prosperity.
20. The Boar represents the Wealth of the Forest; the Pig, Poverty.

THE TWELVE ORNAMENTS
Collectively they represent Power and Authority.

火 **Huo**	粉米 **Fên Mi**	宗彝 **Tsung I**	日 **Jih**	月 **Yüeh**	星 **Hsing**
21. Flames	**22. Rice Grains**	**23. Goblets**	**24. Sun**	**25. Moon**	**26. Stars**

21. Flames represent the Spirit of Fire, Heat, the *Yang* Principle.
22, Rice or Millet is the symbol of Prosperity and Fertility.
23. The Pair of Goblets represent Ceremonials and Sacrifice.
24. The Sun with the 3 Legged Raven is a symbol of *Yang* Principle, Male, Imperial Sovereignty, Brightness.
25. The Moon with Hare pounding the Elixir of Life in a Mortar, a symbol of the *Yin* Principle, Female, Passiveness, Sacrifice.
26. The Stars represent China and the Heart of the Emperor, the Inexhaustable Source of Pardon and Love.

黼 or 斧 **Fu**	黻 **Fu** or 亞 **Ya**	山 **Shan**	藻 **Tsao**	藻 **Tsao**	野雞 **Yeh Chi**
27. Axe	**28. Bows**	**29. Mountains**	**30. Pondweed**	**31. Pondweed**	**32. Pheasant**

27. The Axe represents Justice, Authority. Emblem of *Lu Pan* 魯班 God of Carpenters, also the symbol of Go-betweens.
28. The Conventional Bows or folded Embroidered Alter Cloth is a symbol of Peaceful Collaboration, Embroidery as a Fine Art.
29. Mountains represent a Place of Worship.
30, 31. Pondweed or Waterweed is a symbol of the Spirit of Waters.
32. The Pheasant represents Beauty and Good Fortune, an attribute of the great Emperor *Yü*. The Golden Pheasant pertains to Civil Officials 2nd Grade; the Silver Pheasant, to 5th Grade Officials. The Dragon is also one of the 12 Ornaments. See no. 46.

竹 Chu
33. Bamboo

松 Sung
34. Pine Tree

花籃 Hua Lang
35. Flower B'skt.

靈芝 Ling Chih
36. Fungus

葫蘆 Hu Lu
37. Gourd

33, 34. The Bamboo and Pine are both symbols of Longevity.

35. A Basket of Flowers is the emblem of *Lan Ts'ai-ho* of the Eight Immortals (#104). Also a symbol of Old Age.

36. The Sacred Fungus is a symbol of Immortality and Longevity.

37. The Gourd represents Mystery, Necromancy, Longevity, Science, Medicine, Science of Magic. A charm to ward off Evil Influence. Emblem of *Li T'ieh-Kuai* of the Eight Immortals (#107).

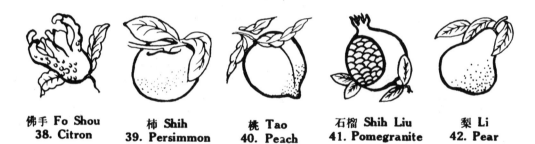

佛手 Fo Shou
38. Citron

柿 Shih
39. Persimmon

桃 Tao
40. Peach

石榴 Shih Liu
41. Pomegranite

梨 Li
42. Pear

38. The Oriental Citron has the appearance of a hand, hence it is a symbol of Buddha's Hand in the gesture of grasping money, a sign of Wealth. Also represents Divine Protection.

39. The Persimmon is a symbol of Joy due to its red color.

40. The Peach symbolizes Marriage, Springtime, Immortality, Long Life. The God of Longevity is often shown holding or sitting on a peach (see #158).

41. The Pomegranite represents Offspring, Posterity, and the Essence of Favorable Influences.

42. The Pear represents Purity, Justice, Longevity, Wise and Benevolent Administration.

DRAGONS AND ANIMALS

魚龍 **Yü Lung** 蟠夔 **Pan K'uei** 夔紋 **K'uei Wên**　　龍 **Lung**　　鳳凰 **Feng Huang**　　龜 **Kuei**
43. **Fish-dragon** 44. **Dragon** 45. **Dragons** 46. **Dragons** 47. **Phoenix** 48. **Tortoise**

43. The Fish-tail Dragon represents a Carp changing into a Dragon in ascending a waterfall. Symbol of Passing the Examinations.
44. An ancient form of Coiled Dragon.
45. Fin-footed Dragons or Hydra.
46. The Dragon is the symbol of the Emperor, Eternity, *Yang Yin*, and has many other attributes. See #13. One of 12 Ornaments.
47. The Phoenix represents the Empress, Beauty, Goodness, Warmth, Prosperity, Peace, the Sun, Abundant Harvests, Reason in Government. Rules the Southern Quadrant. Also called Vermilion Bird
48. The Tortoise guards the Northern Quadrant. Represents Longevity, Strength, Endurance. A Messenger to the Human Race.

獅 **Shih**　　豹 **Pao**　　象 **Hsiang**　　饕餮 **T'ao T'ieh** 麒麟 **Ch'i Lin** 蝦蟆 **Hsia Ma**
49. **Lion**　　50. **Leopard**　　51. **Elephant**　　52. **Ogre Mask** 53. **Unicorn**　　54. **Toad**

49. The Lion is one of the 4 Animals of Power and Energy. Same as the *Fo* Dog. Symbol of Valor, Military Officials 2nd Grade.
50. The Leopard is another of the 4 Animals and represents Bravery, Martial Ferocity. Emblem of Military Officials 3rd Grade.
51. The Elephant is the last of the 4 Animals of Power and Energy. Represents Strength, Sagacity, and Prudence.
52. Probably a Waterbuffalo Head, a Sacrificial Animal and a warning against Avarice, Gluttony, Sensuality, Self-indulgence.
53. The Unicorn symbolizes Benevolence, Rectitude. A Good Omen. Symbol of Military Officials of the 1st Grade.
54. The 3 Legged Toad in the Moon which it swallows during an Eclipse. Symbol of the Unattainable and of Money Making.

BIRDS, INSECTS, ANIMALS

蝙蝠 Pien Fu	蝙蝠 Pien Fu	蝴蝶 Hu Tieh	蝉 Ch'an	鸭 Ya	蟋蟀 Hsi So
55. Bat	**56. Bat**	**57. Butterfly**	**58. Cicada**	**59. Duck**	**60. Cricket**

55, 56. The Bat is a symbol of Longevity, Prosperity, Happiness. Five Bats symbolize the 5 blessings; Age, Health, Wealth, Virtue, and a Natural Death.

57. The Butterfly is a symbol of Joy and Conjugal Felicity.

58. The Cicada represents Immortality, Resurrection, Happiness, and Eternal Youth, Restraint of Cupidity and Vice.

59. The Duck is a symbol of Felicity and Conjugal Fidelity.

60. The Cricket represents Courage and Summer.

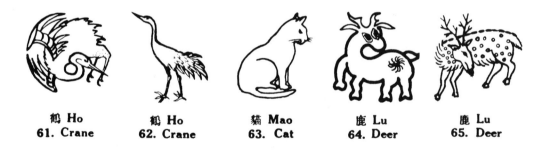

鹤 Ho	鹤 Ho	猫 Mao	鹿 Lu	鹿 Lu
61. Crane	**62. Crane**	**63. Cat**	**64. Deer**	**65. Deer**

61, 62. The Crane represents Longevity and is the bird and sometimes the mount of the Immortals. It aids in communication with the Divinities. Emblem of Civil Officials of the 4th Grade.

63. The Cat is the Protector of Silkworms and Disperses Evil Spirits.

64, 65. The Deer represents Longevity, Official Emolument, Honor, and Success in Study.

FLOWERS OF THE MONTHS AND SEASONS

梅花 **Mei Hua** 桃花 **Tao Hua** 牡丹 **Mu Tan** 櫻花 **Ying Hua** 木蘭 **Mu Lan** 丹灶 **Tan Tsao**
66. Prunus   67. Peach   68. Tree Peony 69. Cherry   70. Magnolia 71. Pomegranite

66. The Prune Blossom is the Flower of the 1st Month and Winter.
67. The Peach Blossom is a Charm against Evil. 2nd Month.
68. The Tree Peony represents the 3rd Month, Spring, Riches, Honor,
    Love and Affection, Feminine Beauty, Prosperity.
69. The Cherryblossom represents the 4th Month, Feminine Beauty.
70. The Magnolia; 5th Month, Feminine Sweetness and Beauty.
71. Pomegranite Blossoms pertain to the 6th Month.

蓮蓬 **Lien Pêng** 蓮花 **Lien Hua** 蓮花 **Lien Hua** 梨花 **Li Hua** 葵花 **Kuei Hua** 葵花 **Kuei Hua**
72. Lotus Pod   73. Lotus   74. Lotus   75. Pear   76. Mallow   77. Mallow

72. The Lotus Pod symbolizes Offspring and Fruitfulness.
73, 74. The Lotus Flower is a symbol of the 7th Month, Summer,
    Creative Power, Purity amid adverse surroundings, Fem. Genius.
75. Pearblossom; 8th Month, Wise and Benevolent Administration.
76, 77. The Mallow is the symbol of the 9th Month.

菊花 **Chü Hua**　　　　　白蟾 **Pai Ch'an**　　　　阿芙蓉 **A Fu Jung**
78. Chrysanthemum　　　**79. Gardenia**　　　　　**80. Poppy**

78. Chrysanthemum represents the 10th Month, Autumn, Joviality,
    Life of Ease, Retirement from Public Office.
79. The Gardenia represents the 11th Month.
80. The Poppy is the symbol of the 12th Month.

THE EIGHT BUDDHIST SYMBOLS

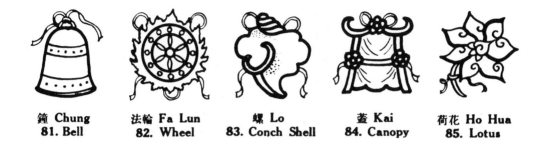

鐘 Chung	法輪 Fa Lun	螺 Lo	蓋 Kai	荷花 Ho Hua
81. Bell	**82. Wheel**	**83. Conch Shell**	**84. Canopy**	**85. Lotus**

81. The Bell implies Respect, Veneration, Signals, Martial Enthusiasm. The Sound disperses Evil Spirits. (An alternate to #82.)

82. The Wheel of the Law crushes all Delusions and Superstitions. A symbol of Buddha's Person, Infinite Changing. Also called the Wheel of Life, Wheel of Truth, Holy Wheel, Wheel of 1000 Spokes, Indestructible Wheel of the Cosmos.

83. The Conch Shell is an emblem of the Voice of Buddha; an appeal to Wisdom, Insignia of Royalty, emblem of a Prosperous Voyage.

84. The Canopy or Flag is a symbol of Royalty, Dignity and High Rank, the Sacred Lungs of Buddha, Spiritual Authority.

85. The Lotus symbolizes Faithfulness. See #s 73 and 74.

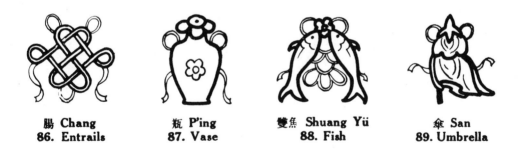

腸 Chang	瓶 P'ing	雙魚 Shuang Yü	傘 San
86. Entrails	**87. Vase**	**88. Fish**	**89. Umbrella**

86. The Endless Knot receives and forwards Abundance, symbol of Longevity, Buddha's Entrails, Infinity, Eternity.

87. The Vase symbolizes Perpetual Harmony, Supreme Intelligent Triumph over Birth and Death A Ceremonial Jar for Relics.

88. A Pair of Fish are a symbol of Marriage, Conjugal Felicity, Fertility, Tenacity. A Charm against Evil.

89. The Umbrella is a symbol of Spiritual Authority and Charity.

BUDDHIST SYMBOLS AND MUSICAL INSTRUMENTS

雷 Lei   珠 Chu   佛足跡 Fu Tzu Chi   寶塔 Pao T'a   Chüan Chang 塵尾 Ch'ên Wei
90. Thunder   **91. Pearl**   **92. Footprint**   **93. Pagoda**   **94. Mace** 權杖 **95. Fly Whisk**

90. Thunder Drums symbolize Revolution and Political Change.
91. The Flaming Jewel symbolizes Pure Intentions, Genius in Obscurity, Feminine Beauty and Purity, the Heart of Buddha. A Charm against Fire.
92. Buddha's Footprint contains the 8 Buddhist Symbols (#s 82 - 89), and others and is a symbol of Buddha's Teachings.
93. The Pagoda is a Receptacle for Relics and secures good Geomantic Influences.
94. The Diamond Mace is a Weapon of the Buddhist Dieties and a symbol of Power and Authority.
95. The Fly-whisk symbolizes the Buddhist admonition Do not Kill, also Magic and Leadership.

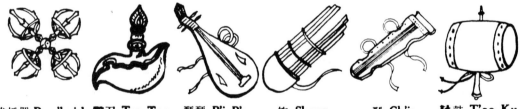

跋拆羅 Po-c'hai-lo 鑿刀 Tso Tao   琵琶 P'i P'a   笙 Sheng   琴 Ch'in   鞉鼓 T'ao Ku
96. Thunderbolt 97. Knife   **98. Guitar 99. Reed Organ**   **100. Lute 101. Hand Drum**

96. The Vajra is a Ritual Scepter and a symbol of Lamaist Power.
97. The Chisel Knife is a Buddhist Sacrificial Instrument, an insignia of Lamaist Dieties, symbol of Sacrifice and Worship.
98. A Guitar shows Determination of the Mind, Purity and Fidelity.
99. The Reed Mouth Organ is the symbol of the Phoenix and the Assembly of the Multitudes.
100. The Lute symbolizes Marital Bliss, Suppression of Lust. One of the Four Signs of a Scholar. See Painting, Checkers, Books.
101. The Hand Drum symbolizes Movement and Ritual Music.

THE EIGHT TAOIST IMMORTALS AND THEIR EMBLEMS
As a group they symbolize Taoism, Transmutation, and Happiness.

Chung-li Ch'üan	Ho Hsien ku	Lan Ts'ai ho	Ts'ao Kuo-chiu	Han Hsiang-tzŭ	Li T'ieh-kuai
102. 鍾離權	103. 何仙姑	104. 藍采和	105. 曹國舅	106. 韓湘子	107. 李鐵拐

102. Chief of the 8 Immortals. Has the Elixir of Life, the Power of Transmutation, symbol of Longevity. Carries a Peach and a Fan to revive the Souls of the Dead.

103. The Female Sage assists in House Management. Her emblem is the Lotus, sometimes is poised on the leaf holding a Fly-whisk.

104. The Patron Saint of Florists, a symbol of Delusive Pleasures. Carries a Basket of Flowers (35), or a Flute (111), or Cymbals.

105. The Patron Saint of the Theater carries Castanets (110).

106. The Patron Saint of Musicians has the power to make Flowers grow and Blossom Immediately. His emblem is a Flute (111).

107. This Sage is a Magician whose emblems are an Iron Crutch and a Gourd (37). Sometimes stands on a Crab or beside a Deer.

Lü Tung-pin	Chang Kuo-lao	鈸 Bo	笛 Ti	魚鼓 Yü Ku	扇 Shan
108. 呂洞賓	109. 張果老	110. Castanets	111. Flute	112. Bamboo Tube	113. Fan

108. The Patron Saint of Barbers is worshipped by the Sick, Slays Dragons and rids the world of Evils. His emblems are the Fly-whisk (95) and Sword (148).

109. This Sage carries a Bamboo Drum. Rode a Mule backwards.

110. Castinets are an emblem of Music and of *Ts'ao Kuo-chiu* (105).

111. The Flute is an emblem of Harmony and of Sages 106 and 104.

112. The Bamboo Drum is a symbol of Longevity and of Sage 109.

113. The Fan indicates Delicacy of Feeling. Emblem of Sage 102.

THE EIGHT TREASURES
Red Ribbons make each a Charm.

錢 Ch'ien
114. Coin

犀角 Hsi Chüeh
115. Horn Cups

艾葉 Ai-yeh
116. Artemisia

方勝 **Fang Sheng**
117. Lozenge

方勝 **Fang Sheng**
118. Lozenges

114. A Cash is an emblem of Wealth.
115. Rhinoceros Horn Cups represent Happiness.
116. The Artemesia Leaf has Healing Properties and is a symbol of Felicity.
117, 118 The Lozenges were used in ancient times to Ornament a a Headdress as a symbol of Victory.

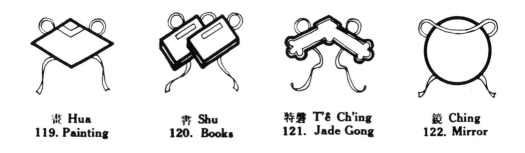

畫 Hua
119. Painting

書 Shu
120. Books

特磬 T'ê Ch'ing
121. Jade Gong

鏡 Ching
122. Mirror

119. A Painting is a symbol of the Fine Arts, Culture, and is one of the 4 Signs of the Scholar. (See #s 100, 132, 155, 156, 158.)
120. Books are a symbol of Learning, and ward off Evil Spirits.
121. The Musical Jade Gong is a Ministerial Emblem and a symbol of the Exercise of Discrimination and of Felicity.
122. A Mirror promotes unbroken Conjugal Happiness and counteracts Evil Influences.

THE FIVE SACRED MOUNTAINS AND OTHER SYMBOLS

恆山 Hêng Shan   衡山 Hêng Shan   嵩山 Ts'ung Shan   泰山 Tai Shan   華山 Hua Shan
123. North Peak   **124. South Peak**   **125. Center Peak**   **126. East Peak**   **127. West Peak**

123. The Northern Peak in *Chili* Province.
    Associated with the Water Element and Black color.
124. The Southern Peak in *Honan* Province.
    Associated with the Fire Element and Red color.
125. The Central Peak in *Honan* Province.
    Associated with the Earth Element and Yellow color.
126. The Eastern Peak in *Shantung* Province.
    Associated with the Wood Element and Green color.
127. The Western Peak in *Shensi* Province.
    Associated with the Metal Element and White color.

波浪 Po Lan   波浪 Po Lan   雲 Yun   磐石 Pang Shih   足布 Tsu Pu   傘 San
128. Waves   **129. Waves**   **130. Clouds**   **131. Rocks**   **132. Coin**   **133. Umbrella**

128, 129. Waves are the Abode of Dragons.
130. Clouds denote Beneficial Rain and Fertility.
131. Rocks denote Permanance and Solidarity.
132. Ancient Spade shaped Coin denotes Riches.
    One of the 100 Antiques.
133. Umbrella to cover Ten Thousand People. A symbol of Respect,
    Purity, Dignity, and High Rank.

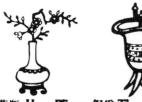 

花瓶 **Hua P'ing** 銅爵 **T'ung Chüeh** 鼎 **Ting** 兒尊 **Fu Tsun** 寶瓶 **Pao P'ing**
134. Flower Vase **135. Wine Cup** **136. Vessel** **137. Wine Pot** **138. Rare Vase**

134. The Flower Vase symbolizes Maintenance of Peace.
135. A Bronze Wine Cup denotes Rank and Ancestral Worship.
136. A Bronze Incense Burner is a symbol of Ancestral Worship.
137. Bronze Wine Pot. The shape warns not to drink to excess
138. A Rare Vase is a symbol of Perpetual Harmony.

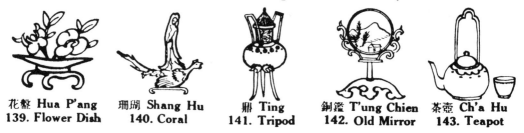

花籃 **Hua P'ang** 珊瑚 **Shang Hu** 鼎 **Ting** 銅鑑 **T'ung Chien** 茶壺 **Ch'a Hu**
139. Flower Dish **140. Coral** **141. Tripod** **142. Old Mirror** **143. Teapot**

139. A Dish of Flowers is symbolic of Beauty and Harmony.
140. A Coral Carving is a symbol of Longevity, Official Promotion. Officials of the 2nd Grade wore Coral Hat Buttons.
141. The Bronze Tripod was an Ancient Ritual Vessel.
142. An old Bronze Mirror heals those who become Mad from the sight of a Demon or Spirit. See 122.

如意 **Ju I** 翎 **Ling** 元寶 **Yüan Pao** 劍 **Chien** 劍 **Chien**
144. Scepter **145. Plumes** **146. Silver Ingot** **147. Swords** **148. Sword**

144. The Scepter is a symbol of Buddha, Magical Powers, Prosperity.
145. Peacock Plumes represent Official Rank.
146. A Silver Shoe Ingot (Sycee) denotes Power and Riches.
147, 148. Swords symbolize Wisdom, Penetrating Insight, Victory over Evil, Superhuman Power, Magic. Emblem of Sage 108.

THE HUNDRED ANTIQUES AND OTHER SYMBOLS

印 Yin, 章 Chang 犀角 Hsi Chiao 筆筒 Pi T'ung Pi, Ting, Ju I   硯 Yen   筆 Pi
149. Seal   150. Horn Cup 151. Brush Pot 152. Rebus   153. Inkstone   154. Brushes

149. The Seal is the symbol of Power and Authority. The Red Impressions cure diseases when applied to open sores.
150. The Rhinoceros Horn Cup symbolizes Happiness.
151. A Brush Holder indicates Scholarly Attainments.
152. A Brush, Gilded Ink Cake, and Scepter form a Rebus meaning May your Wishes be Fulfilled.
153. A Stone for grinding Ink is an Attribute of a Scholar.
154. Writing Brushes are Attributes of a Scholar.

圍棋 Wei C'hi   幅 Fu   書 Shu   壽圖 Shao T'u 臥蠶 Wo Ts'an 蕉葉 Chiao Yeh
155. Checkers   156. Scrolls 157. Books 158. Painting 159. Silkworm 160. Palm Leaf

155, 156. Surrounding Checkers and Books are symbols of Learning. They are two of the Four Signs of a Scholar.
157. Scrolls symbolize Calligraphy, Painting, and Truth.
158. A Painting of the God of Longevity.
159. Recumbent Silkworms, an emblem of Industry.
160. The Palm Leaf is a symbol of Self Education.